Book of pets

SERIF GAMES LIMITED

SERIF HOUSE, HADLEIGH ROAD, IPSWICH, SUFFOLK, IP2 0EE

The fun way to bring learning to life

This book is part of the **Questron** system, which offers children a unique aid to learning and endless hours of challenging entertainment.

The **Questron** Electronic Answer Wand uses a microchip to sense correct and incorrect answers with "right" or "wrong" sounds and lights. Victory sounds and lights reward the user when particular sets of questions or games are completed. Powered by an alkaline battery, which is activated only when the wand is pressed on a page, **Questron** should have an exceptionally long life. The **Questron** Electronic Answer Wand can be used with any book in the **Questron** series.

Questron notes to parents . . .

With **Questron**, right or wrong answers are indicated instantly and can be tried over and over again to reinforce learning and improve skills. Children need not be restricted to the books designated for their age group, as interests and rates of development vary widely. Also, within many of the books, certain pages are designed for the older end of the age group and will provide a stimulating challenge to younger children.

Many activities are designed at different levels. For example, the child can select an answer by recognizing a letter or by reading an entire word. The activities for pre-readers and early readers are intended to be used with parental assistance. Interaction with parents or older children will stimulate the learning experience.

Design   Acrobat Design Limited
Writer   David Smith
Illustrator   Jerry Evans

Printed in Great Britain by BPCC Paulton Books Limited

How to start
Questron®

Hold **Questron**
at this angle and press the
activator button firmly on the page.

Speaker

Questron
use two 1.5 volt
alkaline batteries.
Size AAA

Lights

Sensors
(Keep clean with
a soft brush.)

How to use
Questron®

Press

Press **Questron** firmly on
the shape below, then lift it off.

Track

Press **Questron** down on "Start" and keep it
pressed down as you move to "Finish".

Start   Finish

Right and wrong with
Questron®

Press **Questron**
on the square.

See the green light and
hear the sound. This
green light and sound
say "You are correct".

Press **Questron**
on the triangle.

The red light and sound
say "Try again". Lift
Questron off the page and
wait for the sound to stop.

Press **Questron**
on the circle.

Hear the victory sound.
Don't be dazzled
by the flashing lights.
You deserve them.

Pets' parts!

How good is your knowledge of pets? Look at the picture of a part of an animal. Press Questron on the answer box that shows the correct name of the pet.

| cat | rabbit | hamster |

| parrot | gerbil | horse |

| goldfish | budgerigar | parrot |

| donkey | duck | canary |

| goat | cat | hamster |

| dog | horse | mouse |

| canary | budgerigar | goat |

| duck | goldfish | guinea pig |

| goat | pony | dog |

| donkey | mouse | rabbit |

| canary | rabbit | goose |

Home sweet home

Here are five 'homes' for your pets. But which pet lives in which home?
Press Questron on the answer box that shows the name of the correct
pet for each home.

| dog | parrot | hamster |

| gerbil | canary | fish |

| horse | goat | cat |

| dog | duck | donkey |

| goldfish | cat | mouse |

Noah's Ark

In the well-known bible story, Noah built an ark. In it he put his family and two of every animal to save them from a great flood. Here are some of the animals Noah saved. Many are wild animals. They still live in the wild and find their own food, drink and shelter.

Others are now kept as pets and have to be cared for by their owners. Press Questron on the animals that would make good household pets.

All dogs but different breeds!

There are over 200 different kinds or 'breeds' of dog.
Here are pictures of ten breeds, but which ten?
Press Questron on the correct answer boxes.

bulldog
alsatian
beagle

poodle
boxer
spaniel

dachshund
dobermann
bloodhound

pointer
great dane
spaniel

red setter
basset hound
corgi

retriever
Irish terrier
greyhound

St. Bernard
labrador
wolfhound

foxhound
Afghan
bulldog

corgi
husky
Scottish terrier

saluki
dalmatian
whippet

Working dogs

Although dogs are mostly kept as pets, they have worked with man for many years. Different breeds are good at different jobs. All the dogs on this page make good pets. They are also very good at their jobs. Look at each one and press Questron on the correct answer to each question.

A sheepdog helps the farmer to herd sheep and cattle. The farmer tells the dog what to do by whistling or shouting. Which breed is this sheepdog?

border collie	dalmatian	retriever

St. Bernards are big friendly rescue dogs. They are used to rescue people trapped or lost in mountain snow. Some are trained to find people buried in avalanches. Which St. Bernard is the real rescue dog?

SUNTAN OIL

Some blind people have a guide dog to help them find their way. The breed most often trained for this job is the labrador. What colour stick does a blind person use?

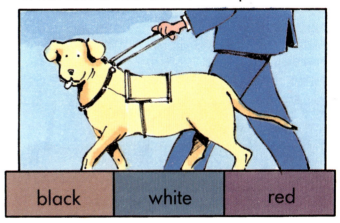

black	white	red

Police use dogs for tracking and to help catch crooks. They use ☐ls ☐ ti ☐ ns because these dogs are strong and intelligent. What is the missing letter?

A	E	O	N

The pointer is a sporting dog that searches out prey for hunters. When the dog finds a game bird it keeps still or 'freezes', pointing its nose in the direction of the prey. Pointers were brought to Britain by soldiers many years ago. Where from?

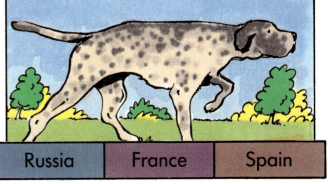

Russia	France	Spain

The do's and don'ts of dog ownership

When you have a pet you must look after it well.
What do you know about caring for a dog?
In answer to the following questions you have to press
Questron on the correct answer, either do or don't.

	DO	DON'T
Make sure your home is big enough for a dog.		
Buy a big dog if you only have a small house.		
Take your dog out for a walk before it has had its vaccinations.		
Keep a lead on your dog when you are training him.		
Praise your dog when he does something right.		
Take your dog for a walk twice a day, or more.		
Put the dog's bed in a cold place.		
Brush your dog for a short time every day.		
Let your dog off the lead when there are cows about.		
Leave the same water in your dog's bowl for a week.		
Take your dog's collar and lead if he goes to kennels so that he can be taken for a walk.		
Be very kind and patient with your dog.		

How many did you get right out of 12?

| 0 – 6 | Buy a dog book. | 7 – 10 | Good | 11 or 12 | Excellent |

Help Peter the puppy find his way home

Peter the puppy has been naughty and run off. Now he wants to go home. Help Peter find a safe route across rough country and back to his kennel.

START

Cat calls

Cats make ideal pets. Cats clean themselves, exercise themselves and some go in and out of the house through a cat-flap. There are many kinds, both long-haired and short-haired.

Track Questron on the letters in each maze that spell the names of five popular cats.

Kwik kat kwiz

How much do you know about cats? See if you can answer the questions below.

When a kitten is born it feeds from its mother's milk. How long must the kitten stay with the mother?

7 weeks   7 months   7 years

When they are born kittens can neither see nor hear. About how long is it before they can?

10 days   10 weeks   10 minutes

What are cats good at catching?

dogs   mice   colds

Which cat smiled a lot in 'Alice in Wonderland'?

Cheshire cat   Lancashire cat   Puss in boots

When a cat has its back arched is it feeling . . . ?

angry

hungry

happy

What does a Manx cat not have?

tail

claws

smell

Over the hurdles

Horses are big and strong and yet very graceful when they run and jump. They need a great deal of looking after and cost more to keep than most other pets. Children keep horses or ponies for riding. Track Questron through the correct answers and over the jumps to win the cup.

START

What is a horse's height measured in?
- metres
- feet
- hands

Horses usually have only one baby at a time. What is a baby horse called?
- buck
- foal
- puppy

What is the smallest British pony?
- New Forest
- Dartmoor
- Shetland

What is another name for a horse's back legs?
- after legs
- hind legs
- reverse legs

There are sporting events that feature horses. What is the name that describes these? (It comes from the Latin name for a horse.)
- bovine
- equine
- canine

Donkey Derby

Track Questron round the racecourse from the start to the winning post as quickly as possible. If you fail to take a corner properly or hit a jump you will get a negative sound and must start again! Play it with your friends or by yourself to find the fastest time.

Horses at work and play

For many years horses have worked for man. Horses also play an important part in many sports. Look at these horses at work and play, then answer the questions by pressing Questron on the correct answer.

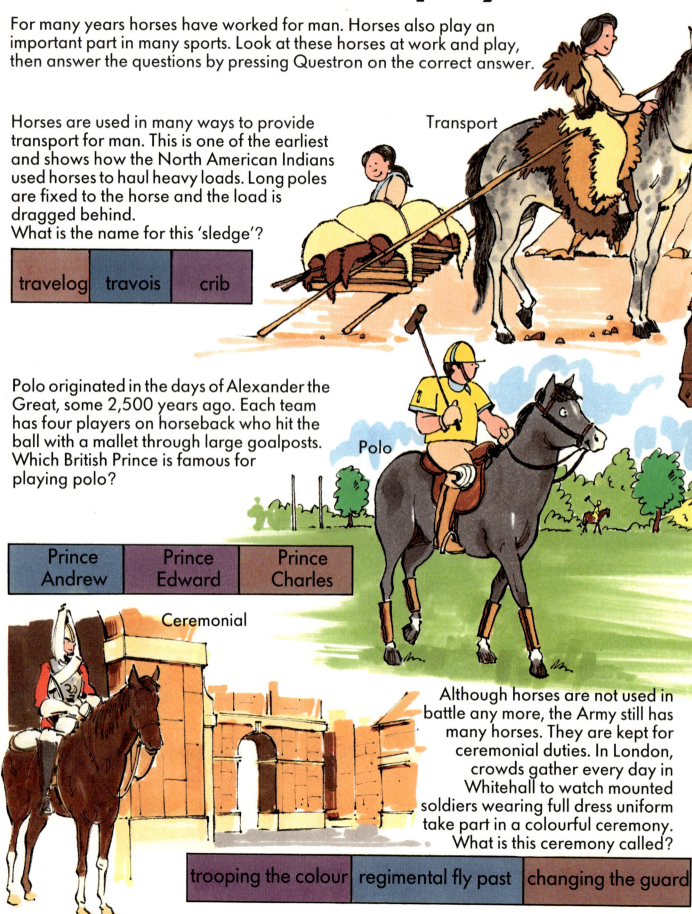

Horses are used in many ways to provide transport for man. This is one of the earliest and shows how the North American Indians used horses to haul heavy loads. Long poles are fixed to the horse and the load is dragged behind.
What is the name for this 'sledge'?

travelog	travois	crib

Transport

Polo originated in the days of Alexander the Great, some 2,500 years ago. Each team has four players on horseback who hit the ball with a mallet through large goalposts. Which British Prince is famous for playing polo?

Polo

Prince Andrew	Prince Edward	Prince Charles

Ceremonial

Although horses are not used in battle any more, the Army still has many horses. They are kept for ceremonial duties. In London, crowds gather every day in Whitehall to watch mounted soldiers wearing full dress uniform take part in a colourful ceremony. What is this ceremony called?

trooping the colour	regimental fly past	changing the guard

Rodeo is a favourite American way of testing the skill of both horses and riders. In one contest a cowboy tries to ride a difficult horse while the horse plunges and leaps in an effort to throw its rider.
The horse is commonly known as a bucking . . . ?

bronco	battler	pony

Rodeo

The very popular sport of show jumping takes place in a 'ring'. The horse and rider have to jump over fences. The jumps are varied and are made to look like hedges, walls and gates. Show jumping tests the skill of both horses and rider. What is the name for the 'irons' the rider's feet are in?

saddle	bridle	stirrups

Jumping

Heavy, very strong horses are used for farm work. The most common farm horse in Britain is the shire horse. It helps with ploughing the fields. The plough is attached around the horse's neck to a . . . ?

harness	straphanger	yoke

Farming/ploughing

17

Goldfish a go-go

Goldfish are members of the Carp family. They are the most popular pet fish in Britain. They can be kept either outside in a pond or indoors in a tank or large bowl. Goldfish vary in colour from bright orange to light gold. Some have black or brown markings. Help this goldfish swim back to his pond by tracking Questron through all the correct answers. Go Go Goldfish.

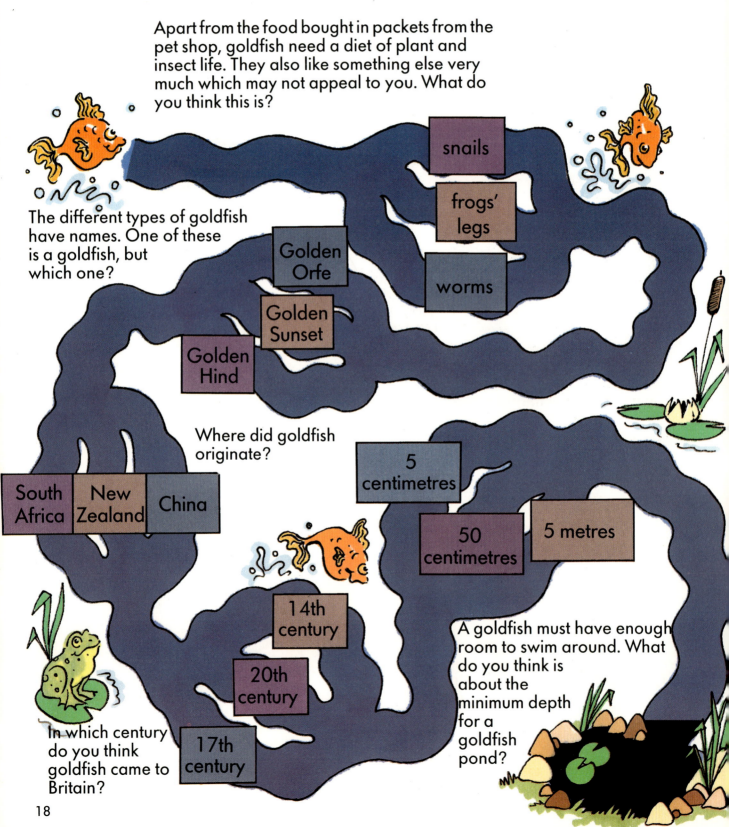

Apart from the food bought in packets from the pet shop, goldfish need a diet of plant and insect life. They also like something else very much which may not appeal to you. What do you think this is?

snails

frogs' legs

worms

The different types of goldfish have names. One of these is a goldfish, but which one?

Golden Orfe

Golden Sunset

Golden Hind

Where did goldfish originate?

South Africa

New Zealand

China

5 centimetres

50 centimetres

5 metres

14th century

20th century

17th century

In which century do you think goldfish came to Britain?

A goldfish must have enough room to swim around. What do you think is about the minimum depth for a goldfish pond?

A fishy story

'Thanks for looking after my fish while I was away,' said Catherine as she collected her aquarium of tropical fish from Nicola.

'Oh, I was pleased to,' replied Nicola. 'I'm glad you had such a nice holiday.'

But Nicola felt a little sad. She really had enjoyed caring for Catherine's aquarium and had become very fond of the fish in the week they were with her. She had talked to them and given them names when she fed them, and they were friends.

'You need cheering up,' said Nicola's mother. 'Let's go to town and visit the Aquarrama. There are fish of all shapes, colours and sizes to see there.'

Nicola had seen the Aquarrama before, but she had never been in to see the fish. Now, with her week's experience of fish care, she felt quite at home in the midst of all the large tanks. Some of the fish had very exotic names, like the red-tailed black shark, the glowlight tetra, angel fish and the pearl gourami, reputed to be one of the most beautiful of all fish.

Soon it was time to leave. As they approached the door, Nicola heard the man in charge whisper to her mother, 'We'll deliver tomorrow, if that's all right.'

'Deliver what? Deliver what?' cried Nicola curiously.

'Your very own fish,' said her mother. 'It's your birthday next week and until today I couldn't think what to buy you,' then she added, 'It's not a large tank, mind you. It's not as big as Catherine's.' Nicola didn't mind. She was very happy and gave her mother a big hug. What a good idea of Mother's.

Press Questron on all the objects in this jumble that appear in the story.

Smallest? Fastest? Largest?

Animals come in all shapes and sizes. Do you know which is the largest, smallest, fastest or slowest? Press Questron on the correct answer for each question.

An eagle is one of the largest birds. An ostrich is bigger, but it cannot fly. Which is the largest of these pet birds?

| parrot | budgerigar | canary |

Which of the animals below do you think is the slowest?

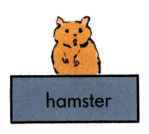  

| hamster | tortoise | guinea pig |

Now which one of these animals is the fastest?

 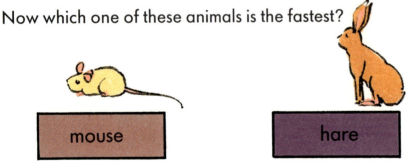 

| mouse | hare | chicken |

Some animals are very brightly coloured and attractive. Others are very plain. This is usually so that they can hide easily. Which of these animals is the most colourful?

| sheep | gerbil | peacock |

Which of these animals lives in the water?

| guppy | dog | pony |

Some animals have misleading names. An example is a Ragdoll. This is not a doll at all, but a cat. Do you know which animal is a Flying Fox?

dog

tropical fish

bird

There is a very popular saying. 'As quiet as a . . . ? Which of these animals is it?

donkey

goldfish

mouse

Which of these pets is the smallest?

rabbit

hamster

cat

Which of these animals has the most legs?

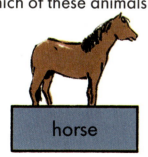

horse

parrot

bat

Which of these pets, when living wild, normally lives under the ground?

goat

rabbit

dog

Furry friends

There are a group of small furry friends we keep in cages at home. These animals, gerbils, mice, guinea pigs and hamsters, are all called rodents. Rodents are gnawing animals. Their incisor teeth grow continuously and they chew and gnaw anything in sight. What do you know about them?
Press Questron on the correct answer to each question.

Which is which?

guinea pig	guinea pig	guinea pig	guinea pig
gerbil	gerbil	gerbil	gerbil
mouse	mouse	mouse	mouse
hamster	hamster	hamster	hamster

Which is larger a guinea pig or a mouse?

| guinea pig | mouse |

Hamsters can be various colours. One colour is by far the most common. Which is it?

| golden | black | white |

What is the average life span of a gerbil?

| 3 months | 3 years | 13 years |

People take about 18 years to grow to full size. About how old is a hamster when it grows to full size?

| 3 weeks | 3 months | 3 years |

Which of these animals is not a rodent?

| dog | rabbit | squirrel |

The tame mice we keep as pets are white and have long tails. Their tails are about as long as their . . . ?

| leg | ear | body |

The mouse trap

Maxi the mouse got out of his cage. He went on an adventure, exploring around the big old house that he lived in. He soon became lost and had difficulty finding his way home. Track Questron from the start right through to Maxi's cage door. You cannot go through any of the walls or closed doors.

Run rabbit run

This rabbit has been out exercising in the garden. More than that, he's been eating the carrots, which he's not supposed to, and the gardener is angry. Now he wants to get back to the safety of his cage as quickly as possible! Track Questron from the carrot patch through the correct answers and back to the cage.

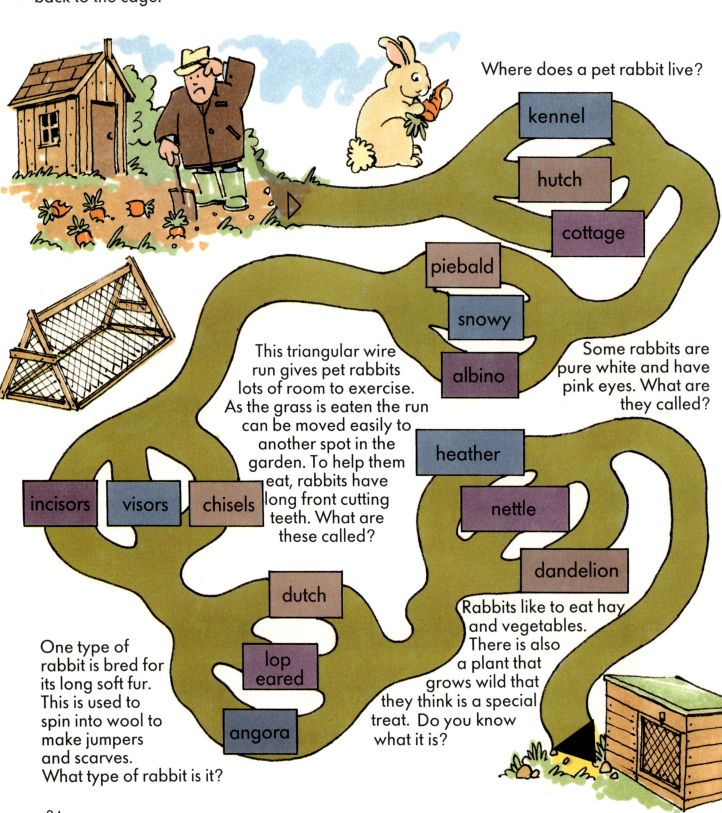

Where does a pet rabbit live?

kennel

hutch

cottage

piebald

snowy

albino

Some rabbits are pure white and have pink eyes. What are they called?

This triangular wire run gives pet rabbits lots of room to exercise. As the grass is eaten the run can be moved easily to another spot in the garden. To help them eat, rabbits have long front cutting teeth. What are these called?

incisors

visors

chisels

heather

nettle

dandelion

dutch

lop eared

angora

One type of rabbit is bred for its long soft fur. This is used to spin into wool to make jumpers and scarves. What type of rabbit is it?

Rabbits like to eat hay and vegetables. There is also a plant that grows wild that they think is a special treat. Do you know what it is?

Bunnies burrow

Rabbits in the wild usually live in groups. Each rabbit digs a tunnel, called a burrow. Lots of burrows connected together are called a warren.
This baby rabbit has been out feeding and has to find its way back home to its mother. Track Questron on the correct route.

rodents

reptiles

Which group of animals does the rabbit belong to?

marsupials

vixen

What is a female rabbit called?

buck

flock

doe

hare

litter

A rabbit has up to about eight babies at a time. This is called a . . . ?

mouse

group

chicken

There is another animal very like a rabbit, but it has bigger ears. What is it called?

10 years

2 years

Very few wild rabbits live longer than about a year. About how long do you think a pet rabbit lives?

5 years

Feathered facts

The main birds that we keep as pets are budgerigars, canaries and parrots. Budgerigars are the most common. Press Questron on the correct answers and see how much you know about budgerigars.

Budgerigars are a small type of parrot and originate from . . . ?

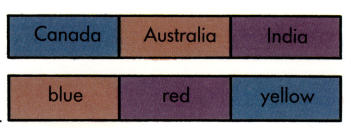

| Canada | Australia | India |

You can tell the sex of a budgerigar by the colour of its cere. The cere is the part at the base of the beak that looks rather like a nose. The female cere is brown.
What colour is the male cere?

| blue | red | yellow |

The correct name for a male bird is a cock. What is a female bird called?

| doe | bitch | hen |

If you keep your budgerigar or canary indoors, its cage should be as large as possible. You should also try to keep two birds together, as one on its own can get lonely.
If you keep your birds in a larger building outside, what is that called?

| pen | sty | aviary |

The budgerigar loses its tail feathers twice every year. Other animals lose their fur or skin. What is this process called?

| releasing | moulting | undressing |

Name that bird!

Here are five pictures of birds we keep as pets in Britain. Track Questron on the letters in each puzzle that spells the name of each bird. Remember you can track up, down and sideways, but not diagonally.

P	A	E	F	S	R
I	R	R	O	M	L
N	C	D	T	G	U

C	L	Y	H	W	K
A	N	A	O	V	T
M	E	R	Y	L	R

B	O	E	R	I	G
U	D	G	W	F	A
S	V	T	X	P	R

C	O	U	T	O	O
R	C	K	A	B	G
M	P	L	S	F	C

T	O	U	P	L	E
H	M	C	F	Y	V
J	S	A	N	K	R

Billy the goat

Female goats (nanny goats) make good pets and also provide milk. Billy goats (male) tend to be a little rough as pets if there are children around. Billy goats are famous for putting their heads down and butting people when they get annoyed. You have three chances to cross the river and escape from Billy the goat to safety. Remember you can go up, down or across, but not diagonally. If you have not managed to cross the river in three goes consider yourself butted by Billy!

Where in the world

Most of the pets in our homes today came originally from other countries. Many of them take their names from these countries. Look at these animals. Press Questron on the answer box that shows where each animal comes from.

| Turkish | Brazilian | Persian |

| French | Spanish | Irish |

| Welsh | Austrian | Polish |

| Italian | English | American |

| Burmese | Indian | Siamese |

29

A visit to the pet shop

You have to go to the pet shop for food. On your way you have to answer ten questions. Press Questron on the correct answers to reach the pet shop.

1 This book has pictures of ☐ abbits in it. Which letter is missing?

B   R   N

4 Which cat is the Siamese cat?

5 Which dog is called Patch?

sheep   dog   horse

7 Which of these animals lays eggs

8 Which has the longest tail?

9 Which one rhymes with carrot?

parrot   cat   goldfish

2 Where is it safe to walk your dog across the road?

3 If your pet is ill you take him to an animal doctor called a vet. Which is the vet?

6 Which is the duck?

rabbit

chicken

goat

budgerigar

dog

pony

PET SHOP

10 Which of these animals can talk?

There are three series of Questron titles — Little Q, Early Learner and Explorer —
all specifically written to combine learning and fun for a wide range of ages.
Early Learner and Explorer books are designed for use with the Questron electronic
answer wand. The Little Q titles are used with their very own easy-to-handle
Little Q wand (as shown on the inside front cover of this book).

EXPLORER SERIES

AGES 7+

Fact-filled Questron Explorers cover a wonderful range of topics for children to discover and
explore. The colourful 32-page books add an extra dimension to favourite subjects and are ideal
back-up material for school topic work. A great bonus is the full-colour giant wall poster in all
Explorer books.

Titles in the Explorer series

The solar system
Wildlife of the world
Britain's heritage
Peoples of the world
Birds and butterflies
Dinosaur world

LITTLE Q SERIES

AGES 2-5

The bright, colourful titles in the Little Q range help younger children learn the all-important basic
skills they will need before starting school. The activities are designed to be repeated to reinforce
learning and help children remember. They each contain a super pull-out wall frieze.

Titles in the Little Q series

ABC . . .
123 . . .
Counting
Very first words
Early skills
Going to the Zoo

SERIF GAMES LIMITED
SERIF HOUSE, HADLEIGH ROAD, IPSWICH, SUFFOLK, IP2 0EE